POETRY

南風 - Southern Breeze
Dalila Hiaoui and Kuei-shien Lee

Editing by Valerie Guidi

Graphic design and layout by Sara Calmosi

ISBN 978-88-33460-78-9

Ali Ribelli Edizioni
Series – Poetry
www.aliribelli.com – redazione@aliribelli.com

Kuei-shien Lee and Dalila Hiaoui

Southern Breeze
南風

English translation by Paola Antonelli,
Alessandra Carlucio, Jason R. Forbus

AliRibelli Edizioni

To my beloved departed mother Latifa,
grandmother Fatima and her husband, lovely grand-
father Abbas.
It was thanks to you
that my small hands held a book
before even touching a toy!
Dalila

給我逝世的親人、母親拉蒂法、
祖母法蒂瑪、
和可愛的祖父阿巴斯。
感謝您們
要我小手拿玩具之前
先去拿書！
Dalila

Preface

A flow of reflectivity of the consciousness conditioned by the imprint of memories…

Poetry inspired with usual assumptions of the moment of commitment survives within the wave of expectations based on sincere glance towards the past. For the sake of future itself. Dalila Hiaoui is the author of the flow of consciousness and she is creating that within the moment of infirmity. Yes, infirmity of different sending of messages intended towards love unto print on paper of artistry. Thanks to her for that, because her work helps us, the local ones, to understand the world of shadows inside the echo of her Southern breeze.

She is a distinctive poet who follows her quest in a way that does not end in imposed orientations within the search of self in poetry. Often is evident that there are very existence of autobiographical reflections within streams that works as a flood reflects continuous commitment of the author. To whom? To what? First of all, the service for the truth of love and respect for her own mission – the mission of shaping of the sincere reflection of her soul. Messages of hope that aims towards the essence of doing and without a fear she plunges into the text, in her own thoughts, bald or hidden, it does not matter. She scoops the strength to continue within the sincere smile, harsh interlacing of the current and future time.

In search for an echo of her own expectations, inter-weaving of the reality of narratives with imaginary

序

　　由記憶刻印所調理過的意識反射性流動⋯

　　由通常假設承諾時機所啟發的詩、會在對過去真誠瀏覽為基礎的預期浪潮中留存。為了未來本身的緣故。達麗拉．希奧薇是意識流的作者、總是低調進行創造。是的、疏於在藝術領域紙本多方發表的意願。幸賴她、有助於我們局部人員、瞭解她在南風迴響內在的陰影世界。

　　她是與眾不同的詩人、其探索方式並不以在詩學中論述導向自足。往往很明顯、在作品做為豐富反射作者持續承諾的風潮中、的確有自傳性反思存在。對誰?對什麼?首先是、為愛的真理服務、和尊重自己的使命、在於塑造心靈的真誠反射。希望的訊息是針對作為的本質、以自己的思想、無懼地投入到文本中、坦然無隱、毫不在乎。她汲取力量、在真誠微笑中、嚴格交錯現在和未來的時間。

　　在尋找她自己預期的迴響中、將敘述的現實與藝術視域的想像假設交織在一起時、達麗拉開拓無法估量的詩人意圖奇妙區域。同時、她強調偏愛對話、視同童話故事、經常壓抑自己對真誠希望的迴響。

　　首先是因為作者意圖傳達給我們的訊息。讀者只是加以詮釋、也毫不猶豫進行理解、經由整體本質的崩解、尋求個別訊息、但也加以接受。作者在尤其對人類的整合過程中、啟發創新。

　　在尋找答案時、作者探索自我最偏遠的角落。在探索答案時、她追蹤⋯以求喚醒夢想。當然、

assumptions of the artistic visions, Dalila explores the immeasurable regions of wonders of the poet's intentions. At the same time, underlining as a fairy tale, a dialogue preferences, she very often suppress her own echoes of the sincere hopes.

First of all because of the message from the writer that is intended to us readers. Who solely interprets it, but also understand, without hesitating to, through the breakdown of the essence of the whole, seek for individual messages, but also receive them. The author inspires the innovation within the integration. Of the humans, above all.

In search for answers, authoress explores the most remote corners of selfhood. In the quest for answers, she traces… for the awakening dream. Of course, waking up of the being and poetry filled with responses as upgrades in quest. While erases false hopes, not just her own. In the conflict with evil. In herself. And around her. With winning through awareness of her own reality. How? The answers are in her poetry. Open, clear and painfully understandable.

Simplicity of the incidence of understanding of appearance encountering with mature decisions fed by existence so far. Poetry of Dalila Hiaoui is not an accidental deflection of the hitchhiker in the literature, but a posteriori knowledge of creators of the highway of poetic intents.

Poetry presented in front of us reveals the poetess ready to make compromises of audibility and impressions, but not at just all. Namely, the pathos is strange for her. No

喚醒存在和詩、充滿回應、作為探索升等、同時消除假性希望、不僅僅是她本身而已。在與邪惡的矛盾中。在她本身。在她周圍。經由自己的知覺、贏得現實。如何達到?答案在她的詩中。開放、明白和苦心理解。

外表理解投射的簡單、迄今遇到存在導致的成熟決斷、達麗拉的詩不是文學中搭便車的意外轉折、而是創作者在詩的意圖大道上的殿後經驗。

在我們面前呈現的詩、透示女詩人準備好就聽覺和印象進行妥協、但不是全然。意即、她對悲情陌生。儘管她在本質、嚴肅的邊緣加以平衡。

鋪蓋憶念玫瑰的地面、期待本身的最後真相。交織愛的狂熱、悲傷和驚喜、因溫柔而成熟。

用眾多擬人化渴望形容詞、以寓意方式照耀本身的精華、真誠的…命運。與純真編織在一起、加進樂觀主義、就在狂熱意圖的懷抱中、本質蕭然揚升。瘋狂嗎?她在拒絕純粹以奇異灰色混凝土牆建立的樂觀主義環境中、譴責逆行的習慣。謙卑和愛情的詩。全部都是!他們是誰?都是那些被視為是人類、卻不明白可能愛情的具體訊息、即走向幸福的訊息。人的生活就是這樣。走向幸福的基礎。不要阻止。將就吧。當然、希望終究會熄滅。在為未來的新一代建立記憶的同時、甚至立刻就把洪水遺留背後。啊、要是人人都這樣做、一如達麗拉。如果大家願意嘗試。

她正在編織意識可能選項範圍內的本身訊息變數。

matter how she balanced on the edge. Of the Essence. Of Seriousness.

The ground covered with roses of memories expect the final truth about itself.

Interweaved with madness of love, sadness and surprise it matures with gentleness.

With a multitude of personifications aspiring towards adjective, allegorically beaming the pearls of its own, sincere… destiny. Woven with naiveté, optimism is fed while the essence inexorably rising in the bosom of the insane intentions. Crazy ones? Of her environment that denies optimism through building exclusivity with concrete walls of weird gray, retrograde habits to condemn. Poetry of humility and love. All of them! And who are they? It was all of those that are considered humans and not understood the message of an embodiment of possible love, that walks towards the happiness. Human life is that. The foundation that walks towards happiness. Do not stop it. Let it be. Certainly hope dies last. While building memories for the new generations to come, not even for one moment leaves the flood behind. Ah, if everyone would do just like that. As Dalila Hiaoui. If all Would just try.

She is weaving variables of own messages within the possible alternatives, of the consciousness.

As a fighter focused towards the truth (what is the true than the current, historical form of the winning messages) unquenchable tries to give answers to everyday questions of her own libido, of the volition. For the finding of the fulfillment of strange innuendo what calls the life – life.

　　作為專注於真理的鬥士(真實更甚於獲勝訊息的現時歷史形式)、抑制不住嘗試為自己的本能、意志等日常問題提供答案。以便找出滿足稱呼生命為生命的奇異影射。《南風》詩集在此方面的作為已告成功。

　　有待我們繼續尋找自我、並擁有確實在讀者心中所刻印訊息詩情的影射。相信在達麗拉心中、愛是唯一選項(Amor vincit omnia)、以對行動真相的微妙承諾具體表現、因為她以真正…愛情、寫作時、得救了。就是這樣。

　　儘管大膽持續不斷試圖放進她在最終目標訊息中的出版物內、但出現在她面前的是中性河流、還看不到對岸。為什麼?因為目標訊息並非最重要。旅程才是…一切。而她成功做到了。確實創作訊息。透過詩。

　　為什麼她能達成?由於單純中的複雜性…情感的傳遞。在由記憶刻印所調理過的意識反射性流動內。對我們大家都適用。

薩巴呼定.哈德濟雅里奇
塞拉耶佛
波士尼亞與赫塞哥維納

Her poetry of Southern breeze has succeeded in doing so.

It is up to us to continue to look for ourselves and own innuendos exactly within the poetic of messages imprinted into the minds of those who are trying to read it. The belief that love is the only alternative – Amor vincit omnia – within Dalila is embodied in subtlety commitment to the truth of doing, because she survives while she writes in that very… love. Only then.

Although continuously, and with audacity, is trying to put into her prints within the ultimate goal – the message, in front of her is neuter river of words whose other bank is not in the sight yet. Why? Because the goal – the message is not above all. Journey is… everything. And she does it successfully. Creating exactly – the messages. Throught the poetry.

Why she succeeds in that? Due to the complexity of simplicity… the transmission of the emotions. Within the flow of reflectivity of the consciousness conditioned by the imprint of memories. For us all.

DR. Sabahudin Hadžialić, Sarajevo, Bosnia and Herzegovina

Southern breeze

Poor, slaughtered love,
whenever he stained the floor with blood
unjustly was found guilty,
and accused of being a killer!
After the cruelty drained his goodness,
he burned on the fires of passion
and buried his dreams,
then placed his destiny,
in fact his heart, on the shelf of oblivion,
believing that the sparkle of youth was extinguished,
in truth had vanished,
his goal now was to kneel no more,
not even if caravans and tribes reached him.
Until a southern breeze carried a
scented branch towards him
a branch as never seen before
in the gardens of myth,
it fluttered while observing him and
he could not understand:
was it ordering or requesting?
Did confusion knock at his door?
Or did he throw... far away the lock of his heart?
Maybe a revelation?
Or evidence of a prophecy?
Love, in his glory, scented his floor,
not minding who was guilty or a killer.

南風

可憐、遭到屠殺的愛、
在他用鮮血染紅地板時
就受到不公平定罪、
被指控為兇手！
善心經殘酷消磨後、
他點燃熱情火焰、把夢想埋葬、
然後把命運實際上置放在
心裡、擱在遺忘架上、
相信青春火花
已熄滅、
真正已經消失無蹤、
他如今目標是不再下跪、
即使大篷車和部族到達也不在乎。
直到南風為他帶來芳香樹枝、
以往在神話花園從未見過的樹枝
在擺動中觀察他、他無法理解：
那是命令還是請求？
是在亂敲門嗎？
還是他把心鎖丟…遠遠？
也許是啟示？
或是預言證據？
情人、洋洋得意、在地板灑香水、
才不管誰有罪或是兇手。

As a child

As a child they taught me
And that advice is like an inscription
On the rocks
They taught me that success,
All success
that my ambition should not walk beyond my vision
that my thoughts do not fly in the sky of his thoughts
Because it could be a source of danger
And that my tongue does not pray for anybody
Except Adam
Because life without him drives Eve away from
The battalion of mankind
As a child they taught me
But they forgot
That pride is a spark
Even with holy prayers of rain to extinguish it
In a moment it kindles infernos
To destroy me with them
As a child they taught me
But they forgot that God
Had not written "female" along the pages
Of my destiny.
After childbirth breaks my back
I offer her the womb of discrimination
Only to give them some pleasure
They taught me.... They taught me
As a child.

小時候

小時候他們教我
那種訓勉就像鐫刻在
岩石上
他們教我算是成功啦、
完全成功
我的雄心不應超出我的視野
我的思想不可在他的思想空中飛翔
那可是危險之源
而且我的嘴巴不能為任何人禱告
除了亞當
因為生活上失去他會把夏娃驅離
人類群眾
小時候他們教我
但他們忘記
自豪是一種火花
即使神聖乞雨來澆熄
會瞬間引燃地獄
使我與他們一起燼滅
小時候他們教我
但他們忘記
神沒有在我的命書上
寫明「女性」。
我在生產後背部受傷
供給女兒被歧視的子宮
隨便他們取笑
他們教我⋯他們教我
從小時候。

An Endless Love

I love you as you are...
Why this abject look?!
Why this silence?
Just let my will mould you
and you will see what a work of art you become.
Be wise, be educated,
be pious, be religious
and kneel down asking my blessing
by affirming that only now
you have embraced Islamic religion
Be innovative, oh woman,
be a warrior against injustice,
but surrender to me within the borders of my land
with the testimony of my relatives
What about your past?!
I swear, I do not care,
Why this strange look, oh my beloved?!
I will provoke castigation,
torment and severe judgement
because of your misfortune since you were born.
Oh queen of my pride and caress,
is your beauty a certitude?!
or only imagination?!
Oh damned eyes, but are these men blind?
Get ready my darling!
I will let you forget all your fears
if you had not ridden the waves of dissension

無盡的愛

我愛妳和妳一樣…
為什麼有此不屑目光!?
為什麼如此沉默?
讓我的意志塑造妳
妳看變成多麼藝術品。
聰明、有教養、
虔誠、信宗教
跪下來求我祝福
到如今才肯定
妳已信奉伊斯蘭教
有新思想、女人呀、
成為反抗不公不義的鬥士、
但在我國土疆界內向我投降
由我親戚作證
妳過去所作所為!?
我發誓、我不在乎、
這什麼奇怪表情、愛人呀?!
我會招惹懲罰、
折磨和嚴厲批判
因為妳出生就不幸。
自傲又關懷的女王呀、妳美貌是信念嗎!?
還是想像力!?
該死的眼睛呀、這些是盲人嗎?
親愛的、準備!
若妳未擺脫我海上的不平浪潮
我會讓妳忘掉所有恐懼
當然、妳應該用沉默面紗遮蔽自己

in my sea
certainly you should cover yourself
with the veil of silence
Don't say anything my darling
please
your silence is the sweetest response,
I know as well as you
that you did not live
in such a merciful heart as mine.

親愛的、什麼都不要說
請妳
妳的沉默就是最甜美的回應、
我和妳一樣清楚
妳不像我活在
如此慈悲的心中

Who am I?

Oh God!
Am I a woman?
or a labyrinth
of marvels and gifts
into which sorrow
hesitantly peeps?
Oh God!
Am I a woman?
or some insomnia..
fissures
and languor spots?
The heart is beating...
but what did it build..
from dreams?
Oh God!
Am I a woman?
Or a dawn embroidering its life
through different ages...
and a destiny
yes, a miserable one
which doesn't go forward
and doesn't come back
I...I...Oh Adam...
Who am I?

我是誰呀？

天呀！
我是女人嗎？
或是奇景
和才華的迷宮
悲傷在猶豫
窺探？
天呀！
我是女人嗎？
或者有些失眠…
分裂症
和倦怠斑點？
心在跳…
但用什麼建造？
夢想嗎？
天呀！
我是女人嗎？
或是曙光經不同年代
刺繡生命…
和命運
對、悲慘的命運
不會前進
也不會回頭
我…我…哦、亞當呀…
我是誰呀？

Unbreakable passion

Here I am, returning to you,
oh marvellous love
To live your passion from Monday to Friday
How much I missed your words,
while struggling between gridlock and headroom
In front of the children I appear a lion,
while they study and revise
But behind their mum I am a gentle lamb,
even submissive
An adjective, a predicate, an oblique
case, an indirect object of company
and means but never a subject!
The silence of your phone is so sweet,
so marvellous and creative your composure
It is like a musical note. Oh enchantress, I
know but unfortunately I cannot hear it!
Remain endearing for me, giving
me life, support me!
Love me, love me, I am not a fool to
break such a thread of passion…

斷不了的熱情

我來啦、回到你身邊、
奇妙的愛情呀
從週一到週五活化你的熱情
我多麼想念你說的話、
同時在僵局與排除之間掙扎
孩子面前、我扮獅子、
他們讀書和復習時
在他們媽媽背後、我是溫柔羔羊、
甚至百依百順
是形容詞、賓詞、從格、附帶間接受詞、
從來不是主詞！
妳的電話無聲真是美妙、
不可思議且創造妳的鎮靜。
真像音符。美女呀、我知道、
但可惜我聽不見！
請繼續對我甜言蜜語、給我生命、支持我！
愛我、愛我、我不會笨到切斷
一線熱情⋯

Weekend

Oh mother
Do not be astonished
Do not worry for me.
Like in a dream,
when they asked me my age, I answered them:
a weekend.
So serious your smile
It had foreseen impending disaster
and a forbidden conquest.
Congratulations on your perception
I announce my death to you
between the weekend news.
Oh mother
that was my life and this is my death
and at least my heart, satisfied.
Fate is God's will
my pages
are offered in line with destiny
in surrender and submission
Oh mother
within me I was a fool
of love
my eyes poured passion
my eyes poured tears, so touched.
Oh mother
my eyes did not ask for
the same passion

週末

母親呀
不要驚訝
不要為我擔心。
像在夢中、
他們問我年齡、我回答說：
週末。
妳板著臉笑
我預料就要倒楣啦
還會被禁足。
恭喜妳的感受
我在週末新聞之間
向妳宣布我死亡。
母親呀
那是我生、這是我死
至少我已心滿意足。
命運是上帝旨意
我的書本
配合宿命提供
降服又順從
母親呀
我自忖是愛情的
傻瓜
我眼裡熱情盈盈
盈滿淚水、多麼動人
母親呀
我眼中沒有要求
同樣熱情

oh forbear of this love
maybe from it we will see the
flowering of some sprig.
Oh mother
my eyes just need one look
he appeared to me as a moon on
the eve of a celebration,
as the orphans pray for her coming.
A few moments of livableness
would have been enough
as a ceremony
in which the heart danced
and the ribs sang
Oh mother
Every happiness
always concludes with a thunderclap
the lightning flashed, revealing the truth
around me
a barren desert.
Oh mother
so unbearable the globlets of my loneliness
It is a dagger that stains my hip with blood.
The fear to appear in my company
as if I were a dishonour
to hide in the shadow of the curtains
by candlelight.
Oh mother
The honesty of reality is so cruel
and you, oh mother, you know
your daughter and her mercy

要忍受這種愛情喔
由此我們將看到一些樹枝花開。
母親呀
我的眼睛只要一看
他在慶祝前夕以月亮般出現、
就像孤兒為月出祈禱。
片刻宜室宜家就夠啦
像在儀式中
心會跳舞
肋骨會唱歌
母親呀
每次幸福
總是以雷鳴結束
閃電在我周圍
荒蕪的沙漠
透露真相。
母親呀
我寂寞的杯狀細胞多麼難受
那是匕首用血染紅我臀部。
不敢在團體出現
彷彿我是恥辱
被燭光隱蔽在窗簾的
陰影中
母親呀
現實的正直是多麼殘酷。
而妳、母親呀、妳知道女兒
心懷慈悲
所以如果我手中捧著香爐
把丟臉的鏡子摔碎
請不要否認我。

so do not deny me
if I shatter the mirror of disgrace
by kneeling down with the incensory in my hands.
Oh my dear, come to say goodbye to me
and throw me with my glow
worm crown and my pen
into a dark ocean with no return.
Be a witness to my ignorance and madness
In front of my people and of the people of my era.
Oh yes, it only lasts a few weeks, my life.

親愛的、過來向我告別
把我的螢火蟲皇冠和筆給我
丟進黑暗海洋裡、一去不回。
見證我的無知和瘋狂
在我人民和我世代人民的面前。
啊、是的、我的生命只要再活幾個星期就好。

Easy virtue ladies

I am not an easy virtue lady

I would never offer myself
to every thirsty or hungry man:
they just consume a soft body and
drink in brilliant intellect.

I would never offer myself
to a legendary soccer player or a clever hunter:
they always lie and their egos resonate as forcefully
as the loudest drum beat

I am not an easy virtue lady

And whenever I give generously
of myself to someone
he always leaves me, at the end of the night,
That defines a wonderful human being
As he is so hypocritically faithful
to his bridal bed!
I would never be an easy virtue lady.

德性輕浮的女人

我不是德性輕浮的女人

我永遠不會把自己奉給
凡事又饑又渴的男人：
他們只是消耗輕柔身體、
陶醉於聰明智慧。

我永遠不會把自己奉給
傳奇足球員或聰明獵人：
他們總是說謊、自我吹噓
強烈若最響亮的擊鼓聲。

我不是德性輕浮的女人

每當我把自己慷慨獻給某人
他總是在夜盡時離開我、
表明一種奇妙人類
他是如此虛偽忠實於
新娘床！

我永遠不會是德性輕浮的女人

Challenge

Did your heart jump a beat
when I was far away?
Have you ever been enticed
by the idea of moving a trusting step
towards my land?
And you gazed at me...
maybe too long?
How long will you run away
while your heart,
although you suppress it,
is still telling you:
"Don't you know that the phoenix of passion
is a predatory bird?"

挑戰

我遠離時
你是否嚇一跳?
你有沒有動心過
想移動確信的步伐
走向我的土地?
你注視我…
可能太久啦?
你要躲開多遠
雖然心裡
在壓抑
仍然告訴你:
「難道不知道熱情鳳凰
是掠奪成性的鳥嗎?」

My father

I was asked about my father's
untimely death and its causes.
I lost the gist of the speech
my tongue couldn't find the words.
Then I was told:
I'm sorry I raised the subject,
the course of time cannot hide sorrows!
A father's death is a deep wound
and even if we bind it up
the blood flows again and again..

我的父親

有人問起我
父親早死和原因。
我語無倫次
說話找不到字眼。
就告訴我：
抱歉提出這話題、
歷久仍然無法隱藏悲傷！
父親之死是深深傷口
即使好好包紮
還是一再流血不止⋯

Jealousy

You seized me
just as space seizes light
and innocence a child's mouth.
You seized me
in an ecstasy of joy
and deep satisfaction
before a place enveloped us
or an attitude restrained us.
I became, by will, a servant.
You seized me
and I sprinkled my life on your path,
a scent that my bottles of perfume are jealous of.
With the wings of my imagination
I have built houses for you
fenced by the hills of my patience

I have painted you
in my poetry and in my prose,
the master of my time, of my nights.
I made of you my whole day
and my ultimate aim.
I accept your behaviour, you inclinations,
your way of stifling my dumb ego,
your way of shaking off my tear drops
as if they were just grains of sand.
I accept every part of you,
your thoughts as well as your hopes.

嫉妒

你掌握我
像空間掌握光
和天真的孩童嘴巴。
你掌握我
在高興狂喜中
深感滿意
面臨籠罩我們的場所
或是拘限我們的態度。
我自願成為僕役。
你掌握我
我把生命灑在你的路上、
有香水瓶嫉妒的香味。
我藉想像之翼
為你砌造房屋
以我耐心山岡做圍牆。
我用詩和散文
描繪你、
我的時間、夜晚的主人。
我整天培養你
是我的終極目標。
我接受你的行為、你的嗜好、
你抑制我糊塗主觀的方式、
你甩掉我淚滴的手法
好像淚滴只是沙粒。
我接受你的各個部分、
你的想法以及你的希望。
我永遠不能接受的是

What I will never accept
is your jealousy poured into glasses of harshness,
'cause you'hurt me, my thoughts, my chaste hope,
the innocence of girls all over the world,
and the purity of all women,
marking the difference between bless and distress,
between life and its nullification.

你傾注在粗杯裡的嫉妒、
因為你傷害到我、
我的思想、我的樸素希望、
世界各地女孩的天真、
和所有女性的純潔、
標示祝福與哀傷之間、
生活與無聊之間的差異。

I said "I love you"

I said I love you with my overflowing faithfulness
perhaps, my love, I was too impulsive.
I said it while adorning my sad eyes with your love,
I said it before my reserved nature realized it
I said it in a whisper, even before meeting you
and the echo of that whisper became a cry.
Did you care about me and my passion?
Or did your manhood trample
on my noble feelings?
Have you really been the dawn of my tomorrow,
my partner and my best friend?
I elevated your love as a star but
it is setting slowly
so do not hope that further chapters are coming.
This is the story of every free woman
who will never be subdued.

我說過「我愛你」

我滿懷誠意說我愛你
情人呀、也許、我太衝動。
我說時哀傷的眼裡洋溢你的愛情、
我說時矜持天性還沒領悟
我說時低聲細語甚至還沒遇見你
而那低語的回音變成吶喊。
你關心我和我的感情嗎？
還是你的男性本色在踐踏我的高貴情操？
你難道真的是我明日之晨、
我的伴侶和至友？
我提升你的愛如星辰、
但卻慢慢下沈
所以不期望未來還有更多話題。
這是永不屈服的
自由女性人人的故事。

Beauty

Your speech stopped me for a
moment, two indeed!
It bestowed two gifts:
your style instead of your lips
and the pearl drops I would keep in my eyes
that would run down my cheeks, against my
will, while gazing at a silvery full moon.
Beauty fighting against beauty, two indeed!
Beauty on the holy earth adorning
a beautiful dress...
may God protect the first one and the other too.
Oh Lord who created beauty for us...
be merciful to both of our lives.
Its appeal charms us
and if we can escape it once
can we avoid it a second time?

美女

你演講短暫打斷我、誠然有兩次！
奉送兩件禮物：
你的風格、而不是你的口才
我噙在眼裡的真珠液滴
怕在仰望銀色滿月時
不由自主流下臉頰。
美女與美女對抗、誠然是兩位！
聖地美女打扮美麗服裝⋯
願上帝保護第一位還有第二位。
為我們創造美女的主呀⋯
對我們兩人生命慈悲為懷。
其魅力令我們著迷
如果我們能夠逃過一次
有可能避免第二次嗎？

Merciful destiny

They said:
light candles hailing from the universe of repentance,
at night,
the one who left you will return in submission
at night,
giving up pleasure and praying with devotion.
Sail sometimes, in the relentless course of women
and make the melancholy long-lasting.
Dear tribe, I beg your pardon,
I will not stay here,
in this dry and noisy mill that can
no longer irrigate trees.
My lonely heart has lost as much hope
of retrieving a missing love
as of seeing vulgar people
appreciate a box twig.
Destiny is knocking at my door
What can I do if not totally surrender?
Is it easy for us not to bend to the fire from our guts?
These dungeons, these bars, these looms where tents
and hills are weaved.
Eyelashes quickly fluttering towards the skyline,
where the sun rises.
Dear tribe, that's the merciful destiny,
I think its mercy is just
for it is benevolent towards a soul
who is compelled to kneel down through abjection.

慈悲的命運

據說：
點燃來自悔改宇宙的蠟燭、
在夜裡、
離開你的那個人會心甘情願回來
在夜裡、
放棄享樂、虔誠禱告。
在女性固執航程中、有時揚帆
使憂鬱持續長久。
親愛的部族、請原諒、
我不會留在這裡、
在此又乾燥又嘈雜的水磨坊、
不再能夠灌溉樹木。
我孤寂的心已經喪失
尋回失落愛情的太多希望
有如看到平民大眾
欣賞黃楊木樹枝。
命運在敲門
如果我不全面投降、又該如何？
我們容易提起勇氣不屈服火焰嗎？
這些地牢、這些酒吧、
這些編織帳篷和山岡的織機。
睫毛快速向太陽上升的
天際線飄揚。
親愛的部族、那是慈悲的命運、
我認為那慈悲只是
對被迫因卑屈下跪的
心靈表示善意而已

Woman

Each time he said I was his princess
and every time he told me so
my heart was screaming.
I'm his prisoner instead,
in the name of God,
I'm his prisoner.
Oh woman, has not a woman ever
desired to build a palace
or to lead a people,
with or without justice,
or to mould an age according
to her desire.
Oh woman, your greatest desire
was to conquer a heart,
a penetrating gaze.
When you see such, you thank God
and when you feel so, you melt with passion.
Woman, Oh woman, what you desire is only
what I have related.
Then, in the name of your God,
give me a bridge to cross
from you and
towards you.

女人

每次他說我是他的公主
每次他對我說、我的心在呼喊。
我反而是他的囚徒、
以神的名、
我是他的囚徒。
女人呀、還沒有女人渴望建宮殿
或帶領人民、
不論有無正義、
或根據她的願望
編造年齡。
女人呀、妳最大願望是征服人心、
深深看透。
如此觀察時、妳感謝神
如此感覺時、妳融入熱情
女人呀、女人、妳想要的只是
與我相關的事物。
然則、以神的名、
給我橋梁跨越
從你那裡
到我這裡

Don't ask

Please don't ask me about love,
my friend,
'cause I'm bored of it.
Nor about the heart,
oh little sister,
'cause I didn't hold on to it
after it was trampled on.
Don't say, please, that this is
how a lover feels
'cause I loved so much...
I loved...

別問

請別問我情事、
朋友呀、
因為我討厭。
也別問我心事、
小妹呀、
因為被踐踏後
我已經無心。
請別說、這是
情人如何感受
因為我愛太深⋯
我愛

Oh land!

Oh land, your love conquered my soul,
imprisoned my reason, caressed my spirit.
My pride, deprived of shame,
unveiled the secret of your love...
Please, be gentle and tender for a moment...
Because far of you, my heart didn't enrapture
or wander like a gazelle
in the desert of passion.

國土呀！

國土呀、你的愛征服我的心靈、
管束我的理性、撫慰我的精神。
我自豪、撤消羞恥、
揭開你的愛情祕密…
請暫且溫柔體貼…
因為遠離你、我心無狂喜
或者像瞪羚在熱情的
沙漠中流浪

Remember me

Remember me
when I'm far from your eyes,
Remember me
when my fingers touch your hands,
Remember me
when words overflow or dry
on your lips
Remember me
when I'm close and when I'm far
during my lifetime
or on the edge of the grave
Remember me
when a country joins us
or when vast expanses
or the dunes of deserts separate us
Remember me
Remember me
you who took my mind
and made me crazy,
you who diverted my path to your path,
I willingly changed my destiny
to stay by your side.
Remember me
in the morning and at night
Remember me with desire and faithfulness
or with hypocrisy and falsehood
Remember me

記住我

記住我
當我遠離你的眼前時
記住我
當我的手指碰到你的手時
記住我
當言詞在你的唇上
氾濫或乾涸時
記住我
在我一生中
靠近或遠離時
或在墳墓邊緣時
記住我
當鄉土結合我們
或廣闊空間
或沙漠沙丘分隔我們時
記住我
記住我
你擄獲我心
使我發狂
你把我的路轉到你的路上
我心甘情願改變我命運
留在你身邊
記住我
無論早晚
以渴望和忠誠記住我
或以偽善和虛假
記住我

Be noble!

Oh source of sweetness that made
me lose my compass,
my map, my sail and my mast.
You erased my knowledge,
the wisdom of history
and the boundaries of geography
waiting for you or flying to get your magic land
I began to disregard the difference
between hours and seconds
while wandering through love stories
that I found simple and boring.
Be noble if you hug me
and we'll be blessed forever.

要高雅！

甜蜜之源呀、使我
失去羅盤、
我的海圖、帆和桅杆。
你刪掉我的知識、
歷史智慧
和地理疆域
等待你或飛來投入
你的魔地、
我開始勿視
時秒之差
沈湎於感覺單調
無聊的愛情故事。
擁抱我要高雅
我們會永遠獲得祝福

Honestly

Do you really want my heart?
Do you really want me to ride the
cloud of liberty?
I have pity on you, I swear, pity and tenderness!
There is no treason or cleverness
but only what destiny etched on my heart,
line by line...
a heart which is sad among its kinsfolk,
hurt and bleeding in its loneliness,
a dead palm on a dream island...
My heart, and I sincerely declare it,
needs to be cared for, oh dear, it
needs to be mended.
Do you think you can find enough thread
of passion deep inside you?

老實說

你真的想深獲我心嗎？
你真的想讓我騎上自由雲翼嗎？
我憐惜你、真的、又憐惜又柔情！
沒有背叛或巧言
唯有逐行刻在我心上的宿命⋯
那是在親屬間難過的心、
在孤寂中受傷淌血、
夢幻島上枯死的棕櫚樹⋯
我的心呀、我至誠宣布、
需要照顧、情人呀、需要療癒。
你想在你內心深處能找到
足夠的熱情絲線嗎？

Question

This is the last question of a broken heart,
a tired heart, which can no longer sigh or cry...
One day passed by,
and you didn't even ask whether
it is still beating or not
maybe you have forgotten that
according to the law of my heart
a life without you would not be legal.

問題

這是碎心、疲憊的
最後問題、不再嘆息或哭泣…
一天就這樣過去啦、
你甚至不問是否還在心跳
也許你已忘記根據我心中規律
沒有你、生活就是不法

What an arrow

What an arrow,
the one that hit me.
It has dissolved my fixed star
in a second.
It has me dismembered,
melted,
obliterated.
What an arrow
the one that made me forget
myself among my friends.
I could see nothing else
BUT THE LOVELINESS OF TAMSUI:
temples,
and the sunset between the
mountains, and mangroves!
What an arrow
that which has given me
the reins of my existence
beyond my convictions
and social censorship
to take me in a fable
in the legends of genies
giving me joys
never lived before
not even in those moments of
seductive delirium.
What an arrow

好箭

好箭、
射中我。
在一秒間
就解決我固定的星星。
已然把我肢解、
融化、
註銷。
好箭
使我在朋友間
忘掉自己。
我目中所見
無非淡水之可愛：
寺廟、
山間落日、紅樹林！
好箭
賦予我
存在的韁繩
超越我的信念
而社會檢肅
把我帶進
神靈傳說中的寓言
給我前所未有的
快樂
即使在那
心蕩神搖時刻。
畫出來的
好箭

that which has drawn
my passion for Marrakech[1]
to be shared with TAMSUI.

1 Marrakech is my magical city of birth

我對馬拉喀什[1]的熱情
與淡水共享。

1 馬拉喀什(Marrakech)是充滿魅力的城市、作者出生地。
譯按：馬拉喀什是摩洛哥南方重要古都、摩洛哥四大皇城之一。
東方是大亞特拉斯山脈、南邊則是荒無人煙、浩瀚的撒哈拉
大沙漠。雖然地處沙漠邊緣、但氣候溫和、林木蒼鬱、以眾多
名勝古蹟和幽靜園林馳名於世。在柏柏爾語(Berber)中、馬拉
喀什意為「神的土地」。

Oh sea

That's enough strutting in front
of me without considering,
the stiffening of my steps, my time and my path
Gaeta, asleep or swirling
Along the pages of my journeys
I am like you, oh sea
I am calm... calm as a rebel
I weave clothes during fine weather for my tempest
with the surf I carve charms for my ankle band
and amulets for my ring and bracelet
I am like you, oh sea
my cheeks blush
every time the sun visits me.
I am like you, oh sea
I am pregnant with secrets,
persistently hidden by my heart
they are hidden from my breast and appearance
even if everybody exalts the removal of the veil
I am like you, oh sea
my waves are too calm for some ships
they are bridges to connect and
approach peoples and lands
and I eternally embrace, from the
depths of my tranquillity
every discord to attain a sublime musicality
I am like you, oh sea
As you, I do not even repress sorrow.

海喲

毫無疑問、那是足以在我面前炫耀、
我的步伐堅強、我的時間和我的加埃塔[1]
路途、在昏昏沈沈中
循著我的旅遊書籍
海喲、我喜歡你、
我冷靜…冷靜得像反叛者
我在好天氣時為暴風雨編織衣服
以衝浪雕刻我腳踝護帶的飾物
我戒指和手鐲的護身符
海喲、我喜歡你、
每次太陽來探訪我
我臉頰羞紅。
海喲、我喜歡你、
我懷著祕密、永遠藏在心裡
由胸膛隱蔽和表露
即使每個人都讚揚除掉面紗
海喲、我喜歡你、
我的波浪對某些船舶太過平靜
那是連接和趨近人民和土地的橋梁
我從寧靜深處永遠採納
每個雜音以獲得絕佳優美旋律
海喲、我喜歡你、
正如你、我甚至不壓抑悲情。

1 加埃塔（Gaeta）、在義大利拉蒂納省、位於羅馬和那不勒斯之間。

My Red City[1]

They repainted you with blood
oh my dear Red
but they forgot that you'll never be defeated,
in God's will
Bats in the dark cast hell fires
onto your place[2]
believing they could hide your beauty
under mud and ashes,
and that you could no longer evoke
a smile,[3] on every mouth,
or that after their treason you could
no longer enter the heart
of those who can discern your sweetness:
the ascetics and the blind.
May the eye of God protect you, oh my eternal,
you know that your children are lions
and that your seven saints[4] are pillars
so, don't complain and just go, go on.
Since the very beginning you have always

---

1 Marrakech, the red city.

2 Jemaa el-Fnaa, is a famous square and market place in Marrakech.

3 Marrakech is the city of fun and jokes too.

4 The seven Saints or seven men of Marrakech are people who Allah has blessed with a special rank among the Muslims. They were in their times as lights of guidance because of the blessings that Allah showered upon them.

我的紅色城市[1]

他們用鮮血重漆你
親愛的紅色城市呀
但他們忘記你永遠不敗、
按照神的旨意
黑暗中的蝙蝠把地獄之火
丟到妳的場所[2]
相信他們可以把妳的美麗
藏在泥巴和灰燼下面、
妳再也引不起每張嘴的笑容[3]、
或者在他們變節之後、妳無法再進入
那些能夠領會妳甜美的人:
修道者和盲人心裡。
願上帝眼下保護妳、我的永恆城市呀、
妳知道妳的孩子是獅子
妳的七位聖徒[4]是支柱
所以、不要抱怨、就繼續吧。
一開頭、妳就始終是
棕櫚叢中的玫瑰[5]

1 紅色城市指馬拉喀什(Marrakech)、位於摩洛哥南方的重要古都、是摩洛哥四大皇城之一。

2 指德吉瑪廣場(Jemaa el-Fnaa)、馬拉喀什著名廣場和市集。

3 馬拉喀什也是好玩開心的城市。

4 馬拉喀什的七位聖徒是阿拉賜福給穆斯林當中特別位階的七個、因阿拉賜福而成為那時代的鬥士和導師。

5 一首傳統歌曲:馬拉喀什是棕櫚叢中的玫瑰。

been a rose[5] among the palm groves
Tobqal[6] fell in love with your beauty
Ever since "ibn Tashfin"[7] laid your foundation
in the Glory of God, and the troops
of "Al-Gumi"[8] crossed your soil,
and the wise men of "Amazigh's"[9] tribe
reached you.
Andalusia, too, sent its luminaries to you,
"Averroè"[10] honoured your soil,
along with "Lissan ad-din"[11] and
"Ibn Arabi Al Hatimi"[12]

5 A classical song: Marrakech is a rose among palms.

6 Toubkal mountain, is the second highest mountain in Africa after Kilimanjaro.

7 Yusuf ibn Tashfin reigned (1061 – 1106) was leader of the Berber Moroccan Almoravid empire. He co-founded the city of Marrakesh and led the Muslim forces in the Battle of Zallaqa/Sagrajas in Al-Andalus.

8 Abd al-Mu'min al-Gumi (1130 – 1163) was leader of the Berber Moroccan Almohad empire conquered Marrakesh and declared himself Caliph. They then extended their power over all of the Maghreb by 1159. Al-Andalus soon followed, and all of Islamic Iberia was under Almohad rule by 1172.

9 The seven Saints or seven men of Marrakech are people who Allah has blessed with a special rank among the Muslims. They were in their times as lights of guidance because of the blessings that Allah showered upon them.

10 Berbers, Amazigh, the Indigenous people of north Africa.

11 Lisan ad-Din ibn al-Khatib (1313 – 1374) was an Arab Andalusian polymath, poet, writer, historian, philosopher, physician and politician. Some of his poems decorate the walls of the palace of Alhambra in Granada.

12 Ibn 'Arabi (1165 – 1240), was an Arab Andalusian Sunni scholar of Islam, mystic, poet, and philosopher. He is renowned among practitioners of Sufism as "the greatest master" and also as a saint.

托瓦爾山[6]愛上妳的美麗
自從伊本.塔什芬[7]在神的榮耀中
奠定妳的基礎、慕敏[8]部隊踩過妳的土壤、
阿馬齊格[9]部族的賢達來到貴地。
安達盧西亞也把智識泰斗送給妳、
阿威羅伊[10]尊重妳的土地、
加上利桑.迪本[11]和伊本.阿拉比[12]
以及所有遵循至善神光明道路的人眾。

6 托瓦爾山(Tobqal)是非洲次高山、僅次於吉力馬札羅
(Kilimanjaro)。

7 優素福.伊本.塔什芬(Yusuf ibn Tashfin, 統治1061～1106)、是
摩洛哥阿爾莫拉維德王朝(Almoravid)領袖、共同創建馬拉喀什
市、帶領穆斯林軍隊參與在安達魯斯(Al-Andalu)的薩格拉哈斯
(Zallaqa/Sagrajas)戰役。

8 阿卜杜勒.慕敏(Abd al-Mu'min al-Gumi, 1130～1163)、柏
柏爾摩洛哥穆瓦希德王朝(Almohad)領袖、征服馬拉喀什、自
封哈里發。到1159年、權力延伸到馬格里布(Maghreb)、接著
就是安達魯斯、到1172年、整個伊斯蘭伊比利亞都在穆瓦希
德王朝統治下。

9 阿馬齊格(Amazigh)、柏柏爾人在北非的原住民族。

10 阿威羅伊(Averroes, 1126～1198)、中世紀安達盧西亞阿
拉伯的博學者、著作涉及邏輯學、亞里士多德和伊斯蘭哲學、
伊斯蘭神學、伊斯蘭法學馬利基學派、心理學、政治理論、安
達盧西亞古典音樂理論、地理學、數學、還有中世紀醫學、天
文學、物理學和天體力學。

11 利桑.迪本.卡提(Lisan ad-Din ibn al-Khatib,
1313－1374)、阿拉伯安達盧西亞學者、詩人、作家、歷史學
家、哲學家、醫師和政治家。其詩做為格拉納達阿罕布拉宮殿
的牆壁裝飾。

12 伊本.阿拉比(Ibn 'Arabi, 1165-1240)、阿拉伯安達盧西亞
遜尼派伊斯蘭教學者、神祕主義者、詩人和哲學家、在蘇非派
教徒中被尊為「最偉大的大師」、也是一位聖人。

and all those who followed the bright
path of God, the Merciful.
They repainted you with blood, my joy, but
everybody can discern the difference between
the will of God and human treachery!

他們用鮮血重漆、我高興、
每人都能辨識神的旨意和人
類變節之間的差異！

Jerusalem

Oh minarets, uplift the name of God,
Oh bells, ring in the churches
and both laud Jerusalem.
The sun will rise
hence adorn and show yourself.
Placate the opponents
induce them to comprehend the totality,
don't stop until any anger is cast away
away from me, away from you,
together with the wounds which
affect both men and their spirits.
Oh minarets, uplift the name of God,
oh bells, ring in the churches
and both laud Jerusalem.
Make your light, torches and candles be bright
in vigil over mothers whose
children have been killed
and to ease the loneliness of orphans.
Gather the tears rolling down
cheeks, hearts and thoughts
and transform them into necklaces to honour,
with pride and admiration,
all your children who defended you,
like a giant preserving his territory,
only with their kefiah and stones,
their naked breasts, and their empty hand.

耶路撒冷

拜塔呀、揚升神的名字、
鐘聲呀、在教堂響起
都在讚美耶路撒冷。
太陽會上升
就打扮表現妳自己吧。
懷柔對手
引導他們理解整體、
不要停止、直到任何憤怒都拋棄
遠離我、遠離妳、
連同影響男性及其精神的
傷口一起拋得遠遠。
拜塔呀、揚升神的名字、
鐘聲呀、在教堂響起
都在讚美耶路撒冷。
讓你的燈光、火炬和蠟燭燦爛
通宵陪伴遇難孩子的母親
舒解孤兒的寂寞。
承接臉頰流下的眼淚、和心思
串連成項鍊、
以自豪和讚美榮耀給
保衛妳的所有孩子、
像巨人只用頭巾和石頭、
裸胸和空手、
衛護領土。

Contents
索引

Lee Kuei-shien (b. 1937), served as chairman of National Culture and Arts Foundation from 2005 to 2007, now is vice president of Movimiento Poetas del Mundo. He published 24 poetry books, some of them have been translated and published in Japan, Korea, Canada, New Zealand, Netherlands, Yugoslavia, Romania, India, Greece, Lithuania, USA, Spain, Brazil, Mongolia, Russia, Cuba, Chile, Poland, Nicaragua, Bangladesh, Macedonia and Serbia. Awarded with Merit of Asian Poet, Korea (1994), Rong-hou Taiwanese Poet Prize, Taiwan (1997), World Poet of the Year 1997, Poets International, India (1998), Poet of the Millennium Award, International poets Academy, India (2000), Lai Ho Literature Prize and Premier Culture Prize, both in Taiwan (2001). He also received the Michael Madhusudan Poet Award from Michael Madhusudan Academy (2002), Wu San-lien Prize in Literature (2004), Poet Medal from Mongolian Cultural Foundation (2005), Chinggis

Khaan Golden Medal for 800 Anniversary of Mongolian State (2006), Oxford Award for Taiwan
Writers (2011), Prize of Corea Literature of Korea (2013), Kathak Literary Award of Bangladesh (2016), Literary Prize "Naim Frashëri" of Macedonia (2016), and "Trilce de Oro" of Peru (2017), National Culture and Arts Prize of Taiwan (2018).

He was nominated by International Poets Academy and Poets International as a candidate for the Nobel Prize in Literature in 2002, 2004 and 2006, respectively.

李魁賢、1937年生、1953 年開始發表詩作、曾任台灣筆會會長、國家文化藝術基金會董事長。現任世界詩人運動組織(Movimiento Poetas del Mundo)副會長。詩被譯成各種語文在日本、韓國、加拿大、紐西蘭、荷蘭、南斯拉夫、羅馬尼亞、印度、希臘、美國、西班牙、巴西、蒙古、俄羅斯、立陶宛、古巴、智利、尼加拉瓜、孟加拉、馬其頓、土耳其、波蘭、塞爾維亞、葡萄牙、馬來西亞、義大利等國發表。

出版著作包括《李魁賢詩集》全6冊、《李魁賢文集》全10冊、《李魁賢譯詩集》全8冊、翻譯《歐洲經典詩選》全 25 冊、《名流詩叢》30冊、《人生拼圖——李魁賢回憶錄》、及其他共二百本。英譯詩集有《愛是我的信仰》、《溫柔的美感》、《島與島之間》、《黃昏時刻》和《存在或不存在》。詩集《黃昏時刻》被譯成英文、蒙古文、羅馬尼亞文、俄羅斯文、西班牙文、法文、韓文、孟加拉文、阿爾巴尼亞文、塞爾維亞文、土耳其文、馬其頓文、德文出版。

曾獲韓國亞洲詩人貢獻獎、榮後台灣詩獎、賴和文學獎、行政院文化獎、印度麥氏學會詩人獎、吳三連獎新詩獎、台灣新文學貢獻獎、蒙古文化基金會文化名人獎牌和詩人獎章、蒙古建國八百週年成吉思汗金牌、成吉思汗大學金質獎章和蒙古作家聯盟推廣蒙古文學貢獻獎、真理大學台灣文學家牛津獎、韓國高麗文學獎、孟加拉卡塔克文學獎、馬其頓奈姆．弗拉舍里文學獎、祕魯特里爾塞金獎、台灣國家文藝獎

Dalila Hiaoui, a Moroccan national living in Rome, Poet, Writer, and director of the bilingual cultural magazine "Al-Jesr" (the bridge)for literature, Art and Education, and she is a Teacher of Arabic language and culture with the United Nations Agencies and the International University UNINETTUNO, as well as an Arabic proofreader and editor with the United Nations Agencies. she has also a diplomatic experience as a Press translator and a Secretary.

She has 20 publications in Arabic, Italian, English, Serbian and Albanian languages as author and co-author (poetry, novels, prose, play, ect) and she presents the multilingual cultural salon "J'nan Argana" twice a month.

達麗拉.希雅奧薇、摩洛哥國籍、現住在羅馬。詩人、作家、雙語文學、藝術和教育文化雜誌《橋樑》(AlJesr)主任、擔任聯合國機構和國際遠程資訊大學的阿拉伯語言和文化教師、以及聯合國機構阿拉伯文校對和編輯。歷練新聞翻譯和祕書的外交經驗。出版20種著作和合著、有阿拉伯文、義大利文、英文、塞爾維亞文和阿爾巴尼亞文、包括、小說、散文、戲劇等、每月出席兩次多語文化沙龍（J'nan Argana）。

www.ingramcontent.com/pod-product-compliance
Lightning Source LLC
LaVergne TN
LVHW010655200726
843507LV00011B/1887